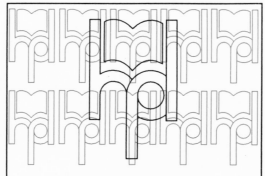

The Turtle Saver

Written and Illustrated by

Laurie Parker

Q QUAIL RIDGE PRESS

For Tracie Holliman Lanphere—
A true friend who has always encouraged me
in my creative endeavors!

Acknowledgments:

Thanks to Sidney Morrow, Mama, Lynn,
and special thanks to my wonderful Quail Ridge Press Family—
especially Cyndi Clark.

Printed and bound in South Korea by Pacifica Communications.
9 8 7 6 5 4 3 2 1

Library of Congress Cataloging-in-Publication Data

Parker, Laurie, 1963-
  The turtle saver / written and illustrated by Laurie Parker.
    p. cm.
  ISBN 1-893062-32-5
    1. Human-animal relationships—Poetry. 2. Conduct of life—
Poetry. I. Title

  PS3566.A6797 T87 2002
  813'.54—dc21   2001048886

QUAIL RIDGE PRESS
P. O. Box 123 • Brandon, MS 39043 • 1-800-343-1583
www.quailridge.com

"Thou canst not stir a flower
Without troubling of a star."

— Francis Thompson
19th Century English Poet

"You must travel throughout
all of time and space
to know the true impact
of any event."

— Thich Nhat Hanh
Vietnamese Poet

happened one June
        on the quiet Natchez Trace:
The start of a chain of events
        that took place.
With one act of kindness,
        that's how it began—
A good deed performed
        by a good-hearted man.

He was driving along, some years back, on his way
To a Little League tournament happening that day.
His grandson was playing. The game was at 3:00.
And he was as proud as a granddad can be.

The ballgame was what he was thinking about
When he spotted an object he couldn't make out.
He saw something dark in the road up ahead.
"Reckon what that is?" he silently said.

Was it just a shadow?
A part from a car?
The man couldn't tell what it was from afar.

But as he approached and came closer to it,
He noticed it moved just the *least* little bit.
And that's when he realized, and cautiously slowed—

A turtle! A turtle was crossing the road!

It lumbered across with a slow turtle's gait.
The man in the truck knew its probable fate.
A car or an RV could squash its shell flat.
It troubled the man just to think about that.

More cars would be coming along soon, he knew.
And so there was only one thing he could do.
He pulled his truck over and stopped right away,
And quickly hopped out—not a moment's delay.

First looking both ways like a smart person does,
He went to the place in the road where it was.
He squatted beside it. "Hello, there," he said—
To which the old turtle retracted its head.

The man picked it up with compassion and care
And walked to a field near and put it down there.
He felt better knowing it wouldn't be struck
And so he went back and drove off in his truck.

And that's just what happened. This good turtle saver
Had done a small creature a very big favor.

And this simple act that was mighty kind-hearted,
Is how several things that took place all got started...

The just-rescued turtle sat still for a spell,
Then finally his head poked back out of his shell.
Not really aware what had happened at all,
He blinked several times, then he started to crawl.
He crawled through the grass where he'd been gently put.
He moved several inches at first—then a foot.
He crawled through that green field. He ambled across
And came to some trees draped with thick Spanish moss.
He entered the woods, then emerged from the trees.
He came to some weeds, and he forged on through these.

He crawled and he crawled, 'til he'd gone 'bout a mile.
Needless to tell you, it took him a while!

And after he'd crawled for a week, and then two,
He came to a reservoir, sparkling and blue.
Its muddy bank beckoned. Its cool water called.
So with one great effort, up to it he crawled.
And that's where the crawling eventually stopped—
When into the water the tired turtle plopped.

The splash that he made when he did this was small.
The waves it created weren't big ones at all.
But this little splash was still somehow enough
To set things in motion. To start up some stuff...

For on an old cypress knee, mere yards away,
A big sleepy bullfrog sat sunning that day.
When he heard the soft splash—the turtle *kerplop,*
It startled him somehow and caused him to hop.
He leapt with great force from where he'd been sitting.
And while he was airborne, he barely missed hitting
A great big ol' dragonfly, aimlessly gliding.

The two critters came very close to colliding!
The quick dragonfly sharply turned in the air,
Avoiding a crash with the frog that was there.

This bug changed directions.
His dodge took him high
Way up, where no bothersome frogs could go by.

Now, what of this close call?
What of this near miss?
Is there some conclusion to draw about this?
Was it only random, or does it make sense
To say it was part of a chain of events?

A turtle is saved, and creates a small splash...
A jarred frog and big bug with wings almost crash...
The dragonfly dodges and heads on up higher...

Did just one good deed help make all this transpire?

For if this one turtle had not been alive,
If he'd not been saved by that man on a drive,
He couldn't have crawled to that lake for a drink.
Would these things have happened?
Now, what do you think?
Would that lazy bullfrog
    have budged from his spot
If there'd been no turtle splash?
Probably not.
Perhaps something else would have made that frog go.
But we just can't say that.
We really don't know.

And what of the dragonfly—now way up high?
It might be important.
Just wait to see why...

The dragonfly liked it up high where he was.
He darted and dashed with his wings all abuzz.
He never had risen so far up before.
There seemed to be more room to sail and to soar.

'Twas while he was up there that something occurred—
Another near-crash! But this time, with a bird!
He'd not seen it coming right toward him at all,
For it was a hummingbird. They're pretty small.

They looked at each other, each holding his ground.
The bird made the first move—a quick, sudden bound.
The bird chased the dragonfly! It was like tag!
They zoomed through the air with a zig and a zag.

This playful pursuit carried on for a bit,
Until the small hummingbird grew tired and quit.
The frolicsome hummingbird-dragonfly chase
Had taken them far from their first meeting place.
And now the small hummingbird realized he'd flown
To some other place that to him was unknown.
He hovered and hummed, and looked this way and that.
Where was that feeder he once had been at?

He saw something red near the ground way below.
And that's where the wee bird decided to go.

Below, far below, in a backyard somewhere,
A woman was sitting outside in a chair.
She sat by herself, sadly wiping a tear.
Her husband had died. It had been a hard year.
She now was a widow, and she missed him greatly.
Just facing each day had been hard for her lately.
She sat doing something that made her more sad.
She looked through an album of photos she had.
The album was big, and its cover was red.
Its full pages spoke of the life they had led.
Their wedding...their children...vacations...and more...
Birthdays...and Christmases...good times galore...
Black and white photos...old portraits now yellow...
Her husband had been such a wonderful fellow.
She stared at a picture, and his handsome grin,
When something made goose bumps appear on her skin:

The hummingbird came down and hovered nearby.
The red of her album had captured his eye.
Just inches away—right in front of her face,
The tiny bird seemed to just float in one place.
The widow sat still without saying a word,
Amazed to have such a close look at the bird.
The bird was so delicate, tiny, and sweet.
She marveled to watch him and see his wings beat.
Her yard had no feeder for this little guy,
And so he took off and flew back way up high.
But she'd been uplifted and cheered by his coming.
The rest of the morning she walked around humming.

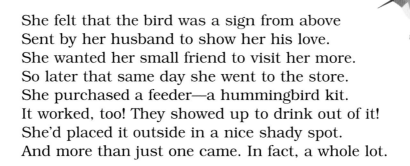

She felt that the bird was a sign from above
Sent by her husband to show her his love.
She wanted her small friend to visit her more.
So later that same day she went to the store.
She purchased a feeder—a hummingbird kit.
It worked, too! They showed up to drink out of it!
She'd placed it outside in a nice shady spot.
And more than just one came. In fact, a whole lot.

She got quite attached to the visiting hummers.
Like jewels with wings, how they brightened her summers!
The joy that they brought her was too great for words.
So one year she started to feed other birds.
She bought several feeders, and all kinds of seed.
She put out old cornbread—it makes yummy feed!
She got a nice birdbath and something called suet.
Birds loved her yard now. They came flying to it.
Robins and redbirds, and jays bright and blue,
And sparrows and finches and woodpeckers, too.

Her yard was a happy place year after year,
With pretty birds singing and chirping their cheer.
The smiles that they gave her were lovely to see...

To think that one hummingbird caused this to be!

If he'd not shown up in her yard on the day
He chased that big dragonfly out of his way,
And if that same dragonfly hadn't flown high
Because of the splash-startled frog going by...
If not for that one turtle saved by the man...

Would she have become such a bird-watching fan?

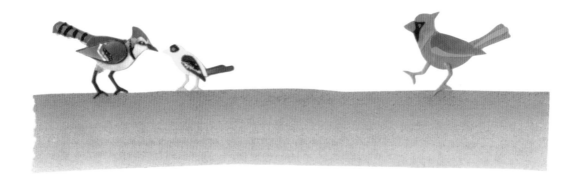

'Bout three blocks away from this bird-watching spot,
On the edge of downtown, on a small corner lot,
Was an old service station, closed down years before.
With two rusty gas pumps that pumped gas no more,
And windows half-broken, and half caked with grime,
It would have been likely a matter of time
Before someone bought it and leveled it flat.
That happens quite often to places like that.
But something prevented it. Something occurred.
Something involving another small bird.

A wren that flew over
    this old place one day
Had been at the widow's yard
    three blocks away.
He'd eaten some seeds there,
    and he never knew
A seed was still stuck to his tail when he flew.
And as he flew over the edge of downtown,
The seed came unstuck, and it came falling down.

The little seed landed in quite a location:
Between those two pumps at the old service station!

This wouldn't have been
    much worth talking about,
Except that the seed the wren dropped
    made a sprout!
From up through a crack in the ground
    it shot through:
A little green shoot.
And it grew and it grew.

And it was a wonder how, as the weeks passed,
The shoot made a green plant that kept growing fast.
Between those two gas pumps, it looked like a weed,
Except it was taller—much taller, indeed!
It peaked at six feet, and then, late in the spring,
A big bud appeared at the top of this thing.
And then something happened that made traffic stop:
A gigantic sunflower opened on top!
The flower was huge and was yellow and bright,
Between those old gas pumps, a curious sight!
People in cars going by slowed to stare,
Wondering, "How did that flower get *there*?"

A man from the newspaper even passed by.
When it came to photos, he had a good eye.
His camera was with him, so he stopped his van,
And took a nice photo, which his paper ran.

It made the front page. It was deemed a rare shot—
A sunflower there in that unlikely spot.
This sunflower photograph cast such a spell,
That other state newspapers ran it as well.
It ran in the *Ledger,* the *Dispatch,* the *Star,*
So lots of folks saw it, both nearby and far.

A single sunflower had caused quite a stir,
But don't forget all that helped make this occur!

In one local city whose newspaper used it,
A wealthy man saw it and quietly perused it.
It wasn't the flower that had him engrossed,
It was the old station he studied the most.
He thought with some work and some love and some paint
The building could be rather charming and quaint.
He bought it and saved it from being torn down,
And now there's a gallery there in that town.
He filled it with all kinds of colorful art,
And gave that old gas station there a new start!

The sunflower photo
just seemed to have power,
And newspaper readers
were cheered by the flower.
One lady who noticed it thought of her sister
And mused, "Since she moved off up North,
I've sure missed her.
I know she loves sunflowers. She would like this.
I'll clip it and save it and send it to Sis."
Her scissors were handy, so with some quick snipping,
She cut out the picture. Now it was a clipping.
She put it on top of her good coupon pile,
Then left to go visit a neighbor a while.

Now, it just so happened that while she was gone,
Her husband came inside from mowing the lawn.
He refilled an ice-water glass at the sink,
And went to the table and plopped down to drink.
A whole lot of things were stacked there on the table,
Catalogs, coupons, the bill for the cable...
A newspaper clipping was lying there, too.
And when the man sat at the table, it blew.
The man picked it up from the floor, never knowing
That it had flipped over. The wrong side was showing!
"What's this?" the man wondered, so he took a peek,
And there was a shot of the "Pet of the Week."
He thought that his wife must have clipped it for that.
The animal pound had a gray tabby cat.
"She's cut out a cat picture...*mmmm...*" the man went,
"Her birthday's tomorrow; this must be a hint.
I know she likes cats. She's been wanting a pet.
She left this right here so I'd see it, I bet!"

He had no idea
that she really had clipped
The flower on back—
'cause the picture had flipped!

He had few ideas
for a gift for his wife...
Muffin tins?
Paperweight?
Swiss army knife?

The man was relieved now.
He knew what to do.
He'd get her that cat and a bowl for it, too!
The very next day, he was off with a bound.
He picked up the cat for his wife at the pound.
He gave her the cat as a birthday surprise.
His wife was delighted. She squealed happy cries.
"Oh, Honey, I *love* it! Oh, what a sweet cat!
Just what in the world made you come up with that?"
Plain tickled to death 'bout her husband's gift choice,
She talked to the cat in a baby-talk voice.
They named the cat "Bubba" right there on the spot,
And Bubba the cat liked his new home a lot.
The husband grew fond of the kitty as well.
He bought him a collar that had a small bell.

Soon Bubba, the last-minute gift for his wife,
Became a big part of their family life.
The couple was glad they'd adopted this pet.
And that's a good thing, but we cannot forget
That Bubba the cat might have stayed at the pound
If not for that clipping the husband had found—
A clipping that wouldn't have been on that stack
If not for the sunflower picture on back—
A giant sunflower that couldn't have been
If not for a seed that was dropped by a wren—
A seed from the bird-feeding lady's backyard...

See the connection? It's really not hard.

It's easy to see, as a matter of fact,
That all that has happened so far can be tracked
Way back to one turtle and one thoughtful act!

Next door to the couple who owned Bubba now,
There lived a young fellow—still single somehow.
He had a pet, also. A bulldog named Daisy.
She was an old dog, and terribly lazy.
She'd mostly just lie around drooling and snoring.
Her long bulldog life had become rather boring.

But Daisy found canine excitement once more
When Bubba the tabby cat moved in next door.

The first time she saw it outside in its yard,
The bulldog went after it, chasing it hard.
So Bubba, with Daisy behind him, went *whoosh*
Through the begonias and hydrangea bush.

The chase took them into a thick grove of pines
Which stood at their owners' back property lines.
The cat climbed a tree, where a dog cannot go,
So Daisy just paced in the foliage below.

This treeing a cat made her feel like a pup,
But, after a while, she grew tired and gave up.
The cat, safely up in that tree, wasn't budging,
So out of the woods Daisy finally came trudging.

She felt mighty proud of her cat-chasing feat,
So like any dog, she went back home to eat.

The coast was now clear, 'far as Bubba could tell.
He came down the tree and went back home as well.

That night, Daisy's owner was watching TV,
With Daisy beside him, content as could be.
They sat on the couch on an old chenille throw
To watch "Andy Griffith," the man's favorite show.
A belly-up bulldog and man—best of pals.
The man rubbed her tummy. He tickled her jowls.
He had no idea that with each single stroke,
He contacted something real bad—poison oak!
His bulldog had brought the plant's oil in with her
From out in those woods, where it got on her fur.

The very next day when he got out of bed,
The man was all itchy. His hands were bright red.
He itched all that morning. He still itched at noon.
He scratched at his underarms like a baboon!
He scratched and he clawed. He was itching like crazy.
"This is so irksome!" the man said to Daisy.

It sounds pretty awful. It seems kinda bad—
This poison oak case that this dog owner had.

But sometimes, a bad thing can turn out to be
A very good thing in the end, as you'll see.

His itching got worse, and he couldn't ignore it.
He went to a drugstore to get something for it—
A small, friendly drugstore on Meadowbrook Drive.
And that's where it happened. Right there on aisle five.
By calamine lotions and cortisone creams,
The nice, itchy man met the girl of his dreams!
The girl was a pharmacist. She was so pretty.
And she was not married! And new to their city!
She also was friendly, and to his delight
She said, "yes," to dinner with him the next night.
They went out on one date, and then on another.
They both laughed a lot, and they clicked with each other.
They went on a picnic. They went to the zoo.
They went to a crafts fair, and crawfish boil, too.

This couple who'd met on a pharmacy aisle
Fell deeply in love after dating a while.
The way they had met was their own special joke:
"It wasn't through Fate—it was through poison oak!"

They kidded about it, and yet, it was true—
That terrible itch played a role for these two.
Would this single guy and his girlfriend have met
If he hadn't caught poison oak from his pet?
And would lazy Daisy have gotten in that
If she'd not been chasing the neighbors' new cat?

The young couple married the very next May.
Their wedding was held on a beautiful day.
Way out in the country, not far from a farm,
The chapel they chose had nostalgia and charm.
They held a reception right there on its grounds.
Ol' Daisy the bulldog was there making rounds.

With dear friends, and music, and good things to eat,
Their big celebration was special and sweet.
The ending was grand. In the late afternoon
The bride and groom left—in a hot-air balloon!
The big balloon lifted and took them up high.
The wedding guests cheered and looked up, waving 'bye.
It floated away at a pace that was slow
And moved through the air over pastures below.

The newlyweds thought their balloon ride was grand.
But something occurred when it came time to land.
The huge bright balloon coming down from the air
Came close to some cows, and it gave them a scare!
Afraid that this thing from the sky meant them harm
They broke down their fence and ran off from the farm!

If not for two people whose love led to vows,
Would such a balloon have come near those poor cows?
And what of those cows breaking out of their fence?

It's just the next link in our chain of events...

Two miles away, that same day, after dark
Some young boys were camping outside in a park.
Their folks were in tents back up over the bluff.
The boys stayed up late doing fun outdoor stuff.
They'd built a great campfire, and had food to fix:
Hot dogs and marshmallows—roasted on sticks!
One boy brought a water canteen on their trip.
They passed it around, and they all took a sip.
Above them, the stars were like bright decorations.
The boys used a chart, and they found constellations.

And as it grew later, their campfire went out.
They had just one flashlight. They passed it about.
Each boy, in its light, told a story he knew—
Weird, scary stories—supposedly true.

The flashlight grew dim, and they all leaned in by it.
The crickets stopped chirping. It got really quiet.
The boys were all spooked as it was—spooked a bunch,
When all of a sudden, they heard a strange crunch.
It came from some bushes real close to the boys.
"Shhh!" said one camper, "Did y'all hear that noise?"
They all sat stone still, then again heard the sound.
Something was rustling and moving around.
One younger boy whispered, "What's over there, y'all?"
"A possum, I bet," said another, "that's all."
They shined their weak flashlight, inspecting a bit.
But they could see nothing. The rustling had quit.
They waited and watched, and one said with a shiver,
"Maybe a gator's crawled up from the river!"

Then, after a while, when they'd just resumed talking,
They heard it again! And it sounded like *walking!*
The boys stood up slowly, all poised now to run.
Something was walking! Or was it someone?
Still hidden by bushes, some big *something* crept.
The footsteps got louder the closer they stepped.
"It's Bigfoot!" a boy cried, "He's gonna come through!"
To which, from those bushes, it answered with, *"Booooooo..."*
It sounded real creepy! It sounded too near!
And one of the boys yelled, "Let's get out of here!"
They all took off running—the whole frightened lot,
Scrambling away from this spooky camp spot!

Those boys really bolted! They scrammed! They skedaddled!
One dropped his canteen as he ran, scared and rattled.
You just might have laughed if you'd seen those boys go,
Especially when you hear what they didn't know!
That last eerie sound they had heard as a *"Boooo..."*
Was not that at all! It was only a *"Moooo..."*
That's right! The "bad" creature that drove them away
Was only a cow who had wandered astray—
Yes, one of those cows the balloon scared that day!
The farmer had rounded them all up but one—
This one missing cow that had made those boys run.

The very next morning it all got worked out.
A park ranger found the cow wandering about.

The cow got returned to its owner and farm,
The sweet, gentle creature had come to no harm.
The boys ate their breakfast, and talked of their scare.
They never found out what had frightened them there.
Was it really Bigfoot? It now seemed like fun.
They'd had an adventure! They told everyone!
And as for the one boy who'd dropped his canteen,
He went back to find it at 7:15.
There it was—where he'd dropped it—right there on the ground.
The cap, on the other hand, couldn't be found.
The boy didn't worry. He'd get a new top.
They had those back home at the sporting goods shop.
The vessel itself was the part to retrieve,
And knowing his parents were ready to leave,
He headed back up with his prized piece of gear
That stayed out all night when he'd dropped it in fear.

A canteen got dropped 'cause of one wandering cow.
This matters at some point. Do you wonder how?

The boy with his canteen, his parents, and brothers
Left the state park and waved 'bye to the others.
While on their way home, they had one stop to make—
Their great-uncle's house, by a beautiful lake.
They'd visit with him, and their aunt, and they'd eat.
The boys were excited, and in for a treat.
They loved their great-uncle, 'cause he was so neat!

He'd once been a sailor. He told the best tales!
The boys loved his sagas of long-ago sails.
He taught them fun place names from lands far away:
Pittenweem...Bundaberg...Perth...Firth of Tay...

Now, they had a story to tell *him* about—
The scary adventure they'd had camping out!
They ran inside quickly upon their arrival
To tell their great-uncle this tale of survival.
They took the canteen in to show to him, too.
They told of the footsteps they'd heard, and the "Boo!"
And after describing in length what occurred,
They asked their great-uncle what he thought they'd heard.
Their droll uncle spoke with a gleam in his eye.
"The Wild Man from Borneo!" was his reply.

Their aunt said, "Pshaw! Boys, of course, he's just pickin'—
Wash up for lunch, now. I've fried you some chicken!"
So all of them went to the next room and ate.
The talk at the table and vittles were great.

Elsewhere, away from the dining room din,
Back there in the room they'd first visited in,
Something took place where it wouldn't be seen,
Something involving that camping canteen.
That open canteen that was found with no top—
That had been on the ground where the boy let it drop,
Had something inside of it, moving about—
A pretty big spider about to crawl out!

In one room, folks passed around tasty stuffed eggs,
While in the next room, something crept—with eight legs!
The spider crawled out of that cap-less canteen.
It scuttled right over a new magazine.

It crept down the table, across the wood floor,
And vanished clear under the hall closet door.
The folks in the next room were all in the dark
'Bout what that canteen had picked up at the park.

And what of this spider now in a hall closet?
How did this happen? Just what helped to cause it?

This spider would probably not be around
If not for a canteen left out on the ground.
And would that canteen have been left out that way
If not for a cow that had wandered astray?
And would there have been
    a loose cow around there
If not for a great big balloon in the air?
And would there have been
    such a hot-air balloon
If there'd been no wedding
    that bright afternoon?

And would that nice couple who married have met
If he hadn't caught poison oak from his pet?
And would that man's pet dog have given him that
If she'd not been chasing the neighbors' new cat?
And would that saved pound cat have been there to chase
If not for the other events we can trace?

That sunflower photo the newspapers ran...

        the flower...

            the seed dropped....

                the bird-watching fan...

                    hummingbird...

                        dragonfly...

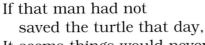

                            frog...

                        turtle...

                            man...

If that man had not
    saved the turtle that day,
It seems things would never
    have happened this way.
A single good deed caused effects
    that have stretched.
It's easy to follow. It isn't far-fetched.
A man saved a turtle,
    and things have progressed
To where a hall closet now harbors a guest...

Several days later, the aunt hosted bridge.
She'd just pulled a red velvet cake from the fridge.
The coffee smelled great—it was ready to go.
She hadn't set up her good card-table, though.
She cleared out the place in the room where she'd set it,
Then went to the hall, to the closet, to get it.

She dreaded the closet because of its clutter,
It needed a cleaning.
The mess made her shudder.
But this time she saw something more than just mess,
A spider was in there!
It caused her distress.
The aunt despised spiders!
She cringed at those critters!
They gave her the willies, the creeps, and the jitters!
It dropped in the hall when she opened the door,
And safely escaped through a crack in the floor.

"That's it!" she declared,
"This hall closet needs work!
This junk's just a place where those spiders can lurk!"

She cleaned out the closet the very next day,
Made piles for Goodwill, and threw some stuff away.
She came across things she'd forgotten she had,
Including a hat that was tattered a tad—
A festive straw hat that was long out-of-style.
Its pink plastic roses and bow made her smile.

Turns out this great-aunt was a grandmother, too,
Who cherished her grandkids, as grandparents do.
She thought of her granddaughter right off the bat,
And said to herself, "She would like this old hat.
She loves playing dress-up and things such as that."

She wouldn't have found this old hat when she did
If not for that spider her hall closet hid.
If it hadn't crawled there from in that canteen,
And grossed out the grandma, and caused her to clean—

It could have been *years* before this hat was seen!

The next time her granddaughter came for the day,
The grandmother gave her the hat right away.
The three-year-old girl put the hat on her head.
"Now, let's have a tea party, Nanna," she said.
This sweet little girl, who loved dress-up and such,
Liked having a tea party, too—just as much!
So she and her Nanna had cookies and tea.
The girl wore the hat, and she giggled with glee!

The hat is important, as you will soon see!

Back at her own house, a while after that,
The little girl got out the fun, fancy hat.
While playing alone in her room, feeling sad,
She thought of the time she and Nanna had had.
She put on some gloves, like her grandmother taught her,
And found the play tea set that Santa had brought her.
She gathered as much as her small arms were able
To carry outside to set up at a table.

She'd brought out some friends for her special affair,
Her floppy flamingo, her rag doll, her bear,
A doll in a bathing suit—brand-spanking new,
And also a cuddly and cute kangaroo.

She lined them all up on a wrought-iron settee
Beneath the magnolia—a nice shady tree,

And there, with that hat on, she served her guests tea!

Just over a hedge,
   right next door to her house,
There lived an old man,
   all alone, with no spouse.
This good-hearted neighbor
   was seventy-eight.
He walked with a cane,
   at a very slow gait.
And even though gardening at his age was hard,
He still grew tomatoes out back in his yard.
The same day the tea party happened next door,
The old man went out to his garden at four.
An on and off breeze blew—quite odd for July.
But it was still hot, and the sun was up high.
He checked to see how his tomatoes were doing.
A worm was on one, so the man started stewing.
He stayed there and piddled too long in the sun.
And this was sure something he shouldn't have done.
The man got too hot, and it made him uneasy.
He felt kind of dizzy and shaky and queasy.
The old man passed out then! He fell to the ground.
And nobody saw. There was no one around.

This man needed help in a very big way.
But how could help come to him there where he lay?

Next door in that cool, tranquil spot in the shade,
The young, happy, hat-wearing hostess still played.
She poured pretend tea in a tiny blue cup
When one of those quick and short breezes came up.
It whipped the big hat
   from the little girl's head.
"Hey! Silly hat!
You come back here!" she said.
She spun around quickly
   and saw her hat fly
And land right on top
   of the hedges close by.
She stood on her tiptoes
   and reached up the hedge,
And touching her hat, knocked it over the edge.
The girl didn't fret. She knew just what to do.
She stooped by a gap in the hedge and crawled through.
And when she emerged on a whole different side,
Her hat wasn't all that the three-year-old spied.

There, on the ground, was the man from next door.
She knew who he was. She had seen him before.
He lay on his back, between rows in a garden.
She thought he was resting, and so she said, "Pardon."
The man didn't answer. The girl cocked her head.
"I'm getting my hat from your yard now," she said.
The man didn't answer, or even say, "Hi."
He lay very still, and the girl wondered why.
She squatted beside him, right there in the dirt,
And finally decided that he must be hurt.
So back through the hedge, to her own yard, she crawled.
She went to her house's screen door, and she called,
"Come outside, Mama! The neighbor man falled!"

An ambulance came for the man right away.
He got help in time, so he made it okay.
He'd gotten too hot, but he bounced back with rest.
And now he's more careful, and that's for the best.
The girl was a hero for what she had done—
First, finding the man, and then telling someone.
But would she have found him passed out there like that
If she'd not gone into his yard for her hat?
And what of that hat that a breeze whipped away?
If she didn't have it to wear on that day...
Would this sweet old man who had gotten too hot
Still be here today? Very possibly not!

It could have been worse for that nice man next door
If not for some other things happening before—
Our chain of events that we cannot ignore.

And what of this old man who had a close call—
For whom things worked out in the end after all?

There's one thing about him that you need to know.
He did something special a long time ago:
He once saved a turtle. A nice thing to do,
And something that should sound familiar to you…
It's all come full-circle. Yes, he's the same man—
The kind turtle saver with whom we began!

The man saved the turtle because he was kind,
And that's where it stopped—that was it, in his mind.
He had no idea when he did this good thing
How many results that his action would bring.

But you know what happened. You've followed it all,
And now you can see—no good deed is too small!

All things are connected somehow, and it's true:
The small acts of kindness, the good things you do
Will all in their time find their way back to you!